OCEANS

RANDY FRAHM

CREATIVE EDUCATION

Designed by Rita Marshall
with the help of Melinda Belter

Published by Creative Education,
123 South Broad Street, Mankato,
Minnesota 56001.

Creative Education is an imprint of
The Creative Company

Photography by Carr Clifton, Com-
stock, Minden Pictures, Peter Arnold,
Inc., and Photo Researchers.

Library of Congress
Cataloging-in-Publication Data

Frahm, Randy.
Oceans / by Randy Frahm.

    p.   cm.
ISBN 0-88682-705-1.

1. Oceans—Juvenile literature.
[1. Oceans.]   I. Title.   93-46807
GC21.5.F73   1997   CIP
551.46—dc20   AC

5 4 3 2 1

Printed in Hong Kong

In Memory of
GEORGE R. PETERSON, SR.

7

Imagine a world with mountain ranges that stretch longer than the Rocky Mountains . . . a world where molten rock rises and spreads over the landscape, only to be sucked back beneath the surface . . . a world in which unusual creatures roam, some so small that a microscope is needed to see them and others so large that an elephant looks tiny by comparison . . . a world that has existed for billions of years . . . a world that is vast, complex, and mysterious.

This exotic world is real. It is the *Ocean*.

The evening ocean.

The ocean covers more than two-thirds of the earth's surface. It is usually regarded as being divided into four main oceans—the Pacific, Atlantic, Indian, and Arctic—as well as many smaller seas, such as the Bering and Coral Seas. When taken as a whole, all of the oceans and seas form a continuous interlocking waterway called the *World Ocean*.

The ocean was created by the same forces that formed the earth more than 4.5 billion years ago. After the earth was compressed out of a cloud of gas and dust, radioactivity made the surface too hot for water to exist. However, the planet did have the elements of water—hydrogen and oxygen—trapped within the molten rock of its interior.

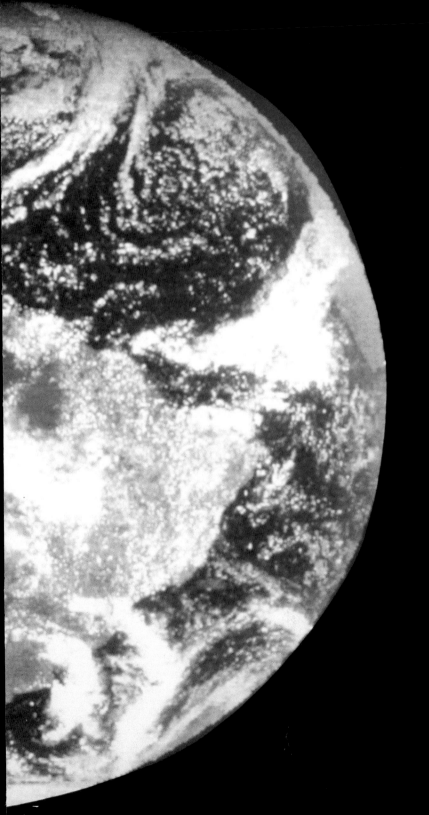

Volcanic eruptions forced the molten rock onto the earth's surface, releasing water vapor into the earth's atmosphere. The vapor remained in the atmosphere until the planet cooled enough to allow the vapor to condense. What followed was a period of severe thunderstorms that drenched the planet with enough water to create the ocean.

As the rain fell, it washed minerals from the land into the ocean. Common among those minerals were sodium and chloride, which combined to make salt. This explains why the ocean consists of *Saltwater*. It is estimated that there are 3.5 pounds (1.6 kg) of salt in every 100 pounds (45 kg) of seawater.

A view of Earth's oceans.

The water of the ocean is constantly changing and moving. Along the coasts, the level of the ocean rises and falls in patterns called *Tides*. Tides are caused by the gravitational pull of the moon, and, to a much lesser extent, the sun. The highest tides, called spring tides, occur about twice a month, when the earth, moon, and sun are aligned and the gravitational pull is at its peak. In most areas of the world, the high or low point of the tide is reached approximately every 12 hours, but in some regions, such as the Gulf of Mexico, a tide occurs only once in 24 hours. The highest tide takes place in Canada's Bay of Fundy in the North Atlantic, where ocean levels change as much as 50 feet (15 m). On average, though, tides only change ocean levels about 2 feet (.6 m).

Tide going out.

Another way the ocean's water moves is in established, consistent streams called *Currents*. Currents can move water considerable distances. The Gulf Stream, for example, begins in the Gulf of Mexico and travels at an average of 4 miles (6.4 km) per hour along the east coast of the United States and Canada until it merges with another established current, the North Atlantic current. Currents are caused by stable, long-lasting wind patterns. They are also caused by differences in the temperature of ocean water. The colder the water, the heavier it becomes. Water sinks or rises, depending on its temperature, and creates currents. Currents are important because they stir the water, distributing nutrients, minerals, and oxygen needed by the creatures that live in the ocean. In many cases, warm currents have a moderating effect on the climate of the lands near which they flow.

Bottlenose dolphins.

The ocean's water also moves in *Waves*. Like currents, waves are caused by the wind. However, waves do not move water from place to place; instead, the waves move through the water like a ripple and the water simply moves up and down. The stronger the wind is, the bigger the waves become. Over time, waves can wear away cliffs and shape coastlines. Wave action also grinds rocks and small pebbles against each other, eventually wearing them down to sand.

15

Just as the earth's surface reveals an infinite amount of variety, so, too, does the ocean floor. Surrounding each continent, where the ocean meets the land, are relatively shallow and narrow regions called *Continental Shelves.* The shelves are usually less than 660 feet (200 m) thick and average 30 miles (48 km) in length.

Surf patterns.

Running alongside certain shelves are *Tren-ches*, areas where one part of the ocean floor tucks beneath another part. Here—not farther out in the ocean—is where the ocean is the deepest. The Mariana Trench, located between the islands of Guam and Yap in the Pacific Ocean, is the deepest part of the ocean. It is about 7 miles (11.3 km) deep. Trenches can be found off Japan, the Aleutian Islands (near Alaska), the Philippines, and the West Indies.

The continental shelves eventually drop off to the *Abyssal Plains*, vast areas of flat ocean bottom. The plains are covered with *Ooze*, a layer of sediment and dead ocean creatures that can be hundreds of feet thick. In some areas the abyssal plains are dotted with underwater mountains called *Sea-mounts*. Created by repeated volcanic erup-

17

tions, seamounts can be miles tall, sometimes breaking the surface of the ocean to form islands. The Hawaiian Islands are the world's largest seamounts.

The plains eventually meet the *Mid-Oceanic Ridge System,* a chain of underwater mountains that circles the earth. These mountains formed over millions of years, when molten material from the earth's core seeped through narrow fissures called *Rift Valleys.* Many of these mountains are still growing, and some extend above the water to become islands. Iceland in the North Atlantic is part of the mid-oceanic ridge.

Part of a rift valley in Iceland.

From the dark depths of the trenches to the shallow, sunlit waters of the continental shelves, the ocean provides a nurturing habitat for an astonishing variety of life. Overall, more than 1.5 million species of ocean plants, fish, mammals, and other sea creatures have been identified. One of the largest birds in the world, the albatross, depends on the ocean, as do reptiles such as the marine iguana and the banded snake. Plant life ranges from the single-celled diatom to the tall, leafy kelp, a giant seaweed that can grow more than 1 foot (30.5 cm) in a single day.

A young albatross rests.

20

Ocean life can be divided into three broad and sometimes overlapping categories: plankton, nekton, and benthos. *Plankton* are tiny plants and animals with very little ability to move themselves. Small as they are, they form the food basis for all life in the ocean. Plankton animals are called *Zooplankton*. They include diverse one-celled creatures called protozoa as well as the young of animals such as crabs or starfish. Plankton plants are called *Phytoplankton*. They, too, are usually single-celled and live in depths of less than 600 feet (183 m), where they absorb light from the sun and nutrients from ocean water. Phytoplankton then convert the light and minerals into energy that is passed along to other life forms in the ocean.

The word "plankton" comes from the Greek word *planktos*, meaning "wandering." Without the means to travel great distances, plankton ride ocean waves and currents from place to place. In fact, their travels impact many other life forms in the ocean. The arrival of plankton in an area usually means larger organisms will follow to feed, which may in turn attract even larger life forms. Sometimes the arrival of plankton can actually light up the ocean. Phytoplankton called *Dinoflagellates* possess the ability to produce light and can give the ocean's waves a pale glow at night.

Diatoms.

Whereas plankton need currents to move, free-swimming organisms classified as *Nekton* are independent of the water's motion. Nekton include creatures as varied as the tiny shrimplike krill, the sea horse, the bottlenose dolphin, the leaping marlin, and the blue whale, at 120 tons (109 metric tons) the largest life form ever to inhabit the earth.

Many nekton have a streamlined shape: the head of the animal is rounded or pointed, with its body widening quickly only to taper at the creature's tail. A streamlined body reduces the resistance animals face as they move through water, allowing them to be faster and more efficient swimmers. Combine that specially shaped body with a powerful method of propulsion, usually fins or flippers, and moving through the ocean becomes easy.

Some animals are capable of astounding speeds. The sailfish, for instance, has a long, pointed snout and a scaleless, extremely streamlined body. Its top fin, called a dorsal fin, folds flat against its body while swimming, and its powerful tail is shaped like a crescent moon. All of these features allow it to slice through water at speeds as fast as 70 miles (113 km) per hour, making it the fastest animal in the ocean.

Sailfish.
Inset: Sea horse.

Not nearly as fast, but just as remarkable, are those creatures that do not have flippers or fins to move them. Squids, for instance, draw water into their bodies, then force it back out. This propels them through the water at speeds of up to 20 miles (32 km) per hour. And there are times when some nekton borrow techniques from plankton. Jellyfish have bell-shaped bodies that move them through the water in much the same way that squids do. But because they also float very well, jellyfish can allow the currents to move them from place to place, sweeping the ocean water with poison-filled tentacles that mean death to the small fish that touch them.

Helmet jellyfish.

Far below the surface lies another part of the ocean filled with life. Plants and animals that live on the ocean bottom make up the category of sea life called *Benthos*. Some, such as crabs, shrimp, and lobsters, creep along the ocean floor, while others, such as sponges, attach themselves to it. Benthos also include mollusks, which are soft-bodied creatures enclosed by a shell, such as clams and oysters. More types of mollusks have been identified than any other ocean animals.

Spotted cleaning shrimp.

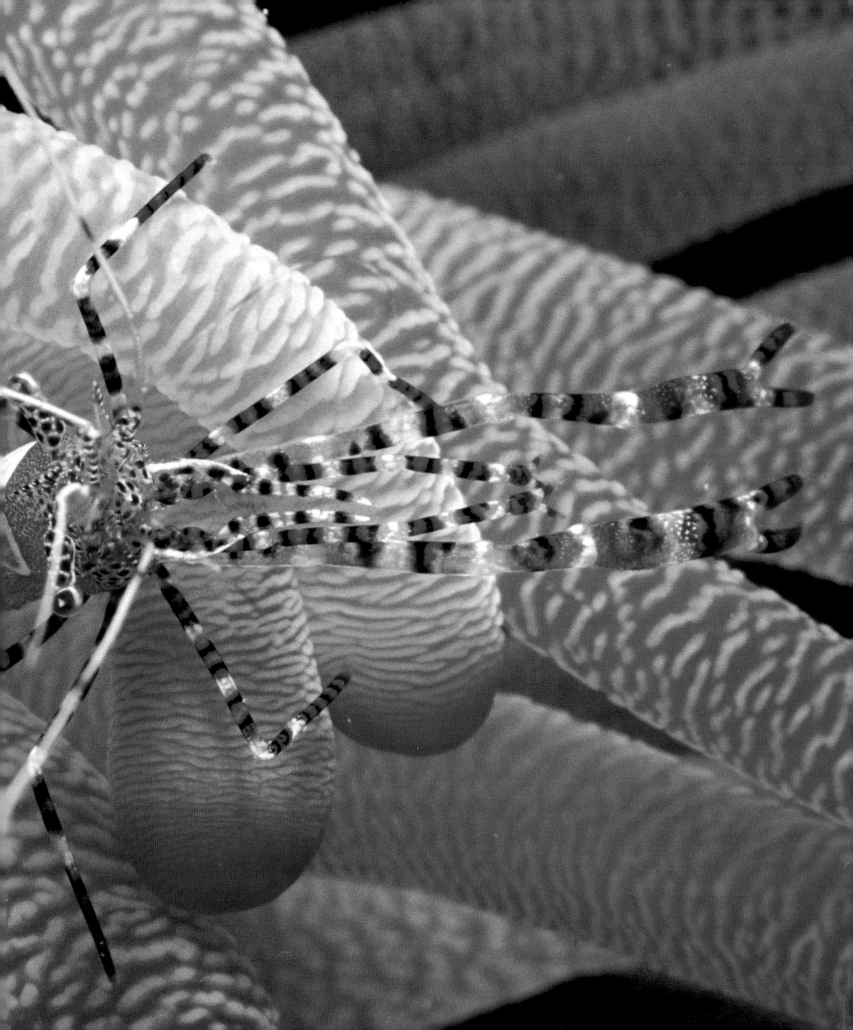

One of the most remarkable creatures in the benthic world is the coral polyp, a small animal related to the sea anemone. The polyps secrete hard, cup-shaped skeletons made of calcium carbonate into which they can withdraw if attacked. When the coral polyp dies, the skeleton remains behind. New polyps connect to the old ones and eventually die themselves. This constant adding of coral skeletons creates intricate and lovely coral reefs. Found in only the warmest of oceans, coral reefs may provide a habitat for thousands of creatures, including shrimp, sea urchins, sponges, starfish, octopuses, and squid. The Great Barrier Reef off the northeastern coast of Australia is the world's largest collection of coral reefs, running more than 1,000 miles (1,609 km) in length.

Great Barrier Reef.
Inset: Coral polyps feeding.

Exotic plants and animals, swirling currents, powerful waves, landscapes buried under tons of saltwater . . . the ocean is all of this, and it continues to change day by day, hour by hour, minute by minute. Much has been learned about this ancient world, but many secrets still float beneath the surface.

~

An astonishing reservoir of life, geological wonders, and breathtaking beauty, the *Ocean* is a vitally important part of our planet, and our relationship with it needs to be one of balance and respect.

A rocky coastline in England.

Index